# Winston Churchill: 94 Fascinating Facts For Kids

*David Railton*

This book is just one of a series of "Fascinating Facts For Kids" books. For more fascinating facts about people, history, animals, and much more please visit:

**www.fascinatingfactsforkids.com**

# Contents

# The Early Years

**1.**   Winston Churchill was born on November 30, 1874, at Blenheim Palace, a magnificent country house in the Oxfordshire town of Woodstock, England.

### *Blenheim Palace*

**2.**   Winston was born into one of England's most famous families. One of his ancestors was the First Duke of Marlborough, a famous general who defeated the French at the Battle of Blenheim in 1704. As a reward, the queen gave him 2,000 acres (3 sq mi / 8 sq km)) of land on which he built Blenheim Palace.

***The First Duke of Marlborough***

**3.**  Winston's father was Lord Randolph Churchill, a rising star in the British government. His mother, Jeanette Jerome, was a rich and beautiful American who became Lady Churchill when she married Lord Randolph.

**Lord Randolph and Lady Churchill**

**4.**   Winston's parents were very busy and didn't spend a lot of time with their son. He was brought up mainly by his nanny, Elizabeth Everest, who was like a second mother to Winston during his parents' frequent absences.

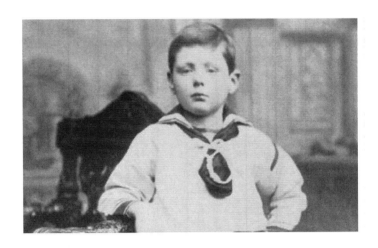

*Winston aged six*

**5.** At the age of seven, Winston was sent away to St. Georges School, a boarding school at Ascot, forty-five miles (70 km) from Woodstock. He hated the school - he didn't do well in lessons and was often beaten for misbehaving.

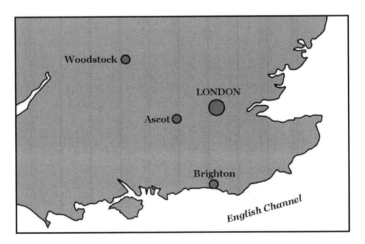

**6.** During the two years he spent at St. Georges, Winston was often ill. It was decided he should be sent to a school in the coastal town of Brighton, where it was thought that the sea air would do him good.

**7.** Winston stayed at Brighton for three years until, at the age of twelve, he was sent to Harrow School, one of the top schools in England. He wasn't a great student at Harrow, although he did win prizes for history and showed a talent for writing.

*Harrow School*

**8.** Toward the end of his time at Harrow, Winston's father decided that his son was not clever enough to follow him into a career in politics. Instead, Winston would join the Army.

**9.**   It was decided that Winston would apply to the Royal Military Academy at Sandhurst, where he would be trained to become an officer in the British Army. He failed the entrance examination twice but passed at the third attempt. Winston entered Sandhurst in September 1893, two months short of his nineteenth birthday.

**10.**   Winston loved Sandhurst and did much better than he had done at any of his schools. After fifteen months of training he graduated eighth out of 150 students, and he knew that the decision to join the Army had been the right one.

# Winston the Soldier

**11.**  After leaving Sandhurst, Winston joined the Fourth Hussars regiment as second lieutenant, and he was soon on his way to India, which was ruled by Britain at the time. He arrived in Bombay (now Mumbai) in October 1896, eager to see some fighting.

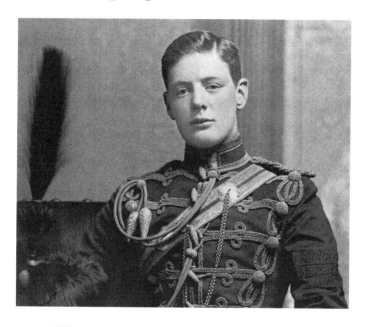

*Winston in the uniform of the 4th Hussars*

**12.**  At first, life in India was unexciting, with lots of free time. Winston used this time for reading and writing, and he read many books about politics, a subject he took a great interest in. But Winston soon became restless and desperate to see action.

**13.** Winston's chance to be involved in some fighting eventually came when he was sent to the India/Afghanistan border, where a revolt against the British had broken out. He spent the next few months fighting the enemy and facing constant danger.

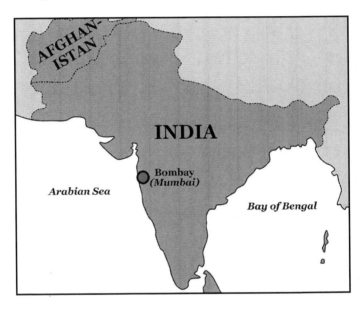

**14.** Along with his military duties, Winston also used his writing skills to earn money. His mother had arranged for him to be a war correspondent for the *Daily Telegraph* newspaper. For every article he wrote, the newspaper paid him £5.00 ($6.50), the equivalent of around £370 ($480) today!

**15.**  Winston spent five years in the British Army and saw action in both India and Africa. During the Second Boer War in South Africa he was captured and taken prisoner. He made a dramatic escape and spent nine days traveling 300 miles (480 km) across enemy territory before reaching freedom.

**16.**  The news of Winston's escape became headline news back in Britain, and when he arrived home in July 1900, he found that he had become a national hero. He was to use this newfound fame to launch his political career.

# Winston the Politician

**17.** At the beginning of the twentieth century there were two main political parties in Britain - the Conservatives and the Liberals. Winston joined the Conservative Party and stood for election to Parliament in the town of Oldham in North West England.

**18.** The people of Oldham turned out in their thousands to hear Winston the war hero give his speeches, and in October 1900 they made him their Member of Parliament – "MP" for short. At the age of just twenty-five Winston Churchill was beginning his political career.

*Winston around the time of his election*

**19.**  Winston had joined the Conservative Party partly because it was the party his father, Lord Randolph, had belonged to, but he soon found that he had more in common with the Liberals.

**20.**  Winston stayed with the Conservatives for four years, often disagreeing with them, until, in May 1904, he left the party to join the Liberals. It was expected that MPs should show loyalty to their party, and the Conservatives saw Winston as a traitor. It would be many years before they would forgive him.

**21.**  Two years after Winston left the Conservatives a general election was held which would give the British people the opportunity to choose which party they wanted to run the country. The result was an overwhelming victory for the Liberals. 397 Liberal MPs – including Winston - had been voted into Parliament, with the Conservatives having just 156.

**22.**  Winston was seen as a rising star in the Liberal party, and in 1908 he was given the important job of "President of the Board of Trade." At the age of just thirty-three he was the youngest member of the government for forty years.

**23.**  Winston loved going to dinner parties and enjoying good food and wine. At one of these parties he found himself sitting next to a beautiful young woman called Clementine

Hozier. They soon fell in love and married in September 1908.

**_Clementine Hozier_**

**24.** In July 1909, Winston and Clementine had their first child, Diana. Over the next thirteen years they had four more children - Randolph, Sarah, Marigold, and Mary; although Marigold tragically died at the age of just two. The Churchill marriage would last until Winston's death fifty-six years later.

**25.** In 1910, Winston was promoted to one of the top jobs in British politics – "Home Secretary." A year later he became "First Lord of the Admiralty" - the head of the British Navy.

**26.** At the time, there was a lot of tension between the countries of Europe. Germany was building a massive army and navy, and the British government was afraid that war would soon break out. Winston's job at the Admiralty was to make sure that the British Navy was strong enough to stand up to the German Navy.

# World War One

**27.**  War broke out in June 1914, and the German Army was soon marching through Belgium to invade France. Britain had an agreement to protect Belgium and declared war on Germany. Other countries also became involved and soon the whole of Europe was plunged into World War One.

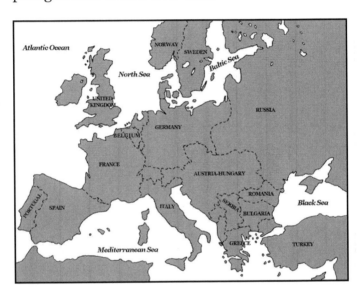

*Europe in 1914*

**28.**  In October 1914, Turkey joined the war on the side of the Germans. Winston persuaded his colleagues in government to send a fleet of battleships to the Dardanelles, a narrow stretch of water that separates mainland Turkey from the peninsula of Gallipoli.

**29.** Winston's plan was for the British Navy to sail up the Dardanelles to capture the Turkish capital, Constantinople. Instead, the Turks sank half the British fleet. It was decided that soldiers would be needed as well as the Navy.

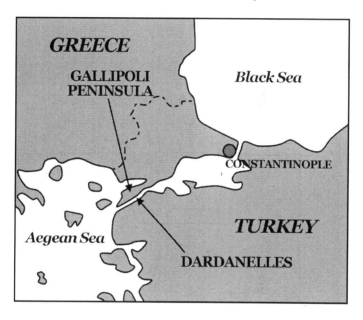

**30.** A force of mainly Australian and New Zealand soldiers was sent to the Gallipoli peninsula in April 1915. But they had been supplied with out-of-date maps and landed in the wrong place. They were attacked by the Turks and suffered dreadful casualties.

**31.** The Gallipoli campaign turned out to be a disaster with many thousands of lives lost. Winston was held responsible for the failure and was removed from his job at the Admiralty. But after the war was over, an enquiry was held which decided that no blame could be placed on Winston for the campaign's failure.

**32.**  Winston still wanted to help his country fight the war and he volunteered to join the Army. He was sent to France to fight the Germans, and he stayed there for six months before deciding to return to Parliament.

**33.**  When he returned to Britain, Winston became part of the government again when he was made "Minister of Munitions," responsible for sending weapons to British soldiers fighting in France. He stayed in that position until the end of the war, when Germany was finally defeated in November 1918.

# Out of Government

**34.** After the war, Winston became "Secretary of State for War and Air," responsible for bringing British soldiers back from where they had been fighting overseas, and helping them adjust to normal life.

**35.** Winston was also involved in giving Ireland its independence. Ireland had been a part of the United Kingdom (England, Scotland, Wales, and Ireland) since 1801, but many Irish people wanted to leave and become a separate country. Winston helped to write the "Anglo-Irish Treaty," which saw the creation of the new Irish Free State - now the Republic of Ireland.

**36.**  In October 1922, the British Prime Minister, David Lloyd George, resigned, which meant that a general election had to be held. It took place the following month on November 15.

**37.**  As the day of the election approached, Winston came down with appendicitis and had to have emergency surgery. He was unable to campaign as much as he would like to try to get people to vote for him, and he lost the election, getting more than 10,000 fewer votes than the winner.

**38.**  Winston was out of Parliament for the first time in seventeen years, but he found plenty to occupy himself. He was a talented artist and he now had time to paint. He also began writing what would be a six-volume, 2,000-page history of World War One called "The World Crisis."

**39.**  Winston and Clementine also bought a new house in the countryside around twenty-five miles (40 km) from Central London. Called "Chartwell," it was a run-down manor house with large gardens, and Winston had fallen in love with it the first time he had seen it.

*Chartwell*

**40.** Clementine wasn't as keen on Chartwell as Winston. She new that the rebuilding would cost a lot of money and that it would be expensive to run. She was right - over the next thirty years Winston spent a small fortune renovating the house and gardens, nearly ruining him financially in the process.

**41.** After two years away from politics, Winston was ready to become an MP again. He re-joined the Conservative Party, and at the next general election in October 1924, he was elected to Parliament once again.

**42.** The Conservatives won the 1924 general election and the new Prime Minister, Stanley Baldwin, asked Winston to become Chancellor of the Exchequer, the second-most powerful

position in the government after the Prime
Minister.

**43.** The Chancellor of the Exchequer is in
charge of the country's money, and the job comes
with a house - 11 Downing Street - next door to
the Prime Minister who lives at Number 10.
Clementine was delighted to live in Downing
Street, but Winston liked to escape to Chartwell
whenever he could.

***Downing Street***

**44.** Winston was Chancellor of the Exchequer
for five years, but at the next general election in
1929, the Conservatives were beaten by the
Labour Party. The Labour Party had been
founded in 1900 and had taken over from the
Liberals as one of the two major political parties.

**45.**   Although Winston was re-elected to Parliament, the Labour victory meant that he was not part of the government any more. He was to spend the next ten years in the shadows and at the age of fifty-five it looked as though his political career was over.

**46.**   Winston again had more time for painting and writing, but he was becoming concerned at what was happening in the rest of Europe. Germany, under the leadership of Adolf Hitler, was once again building a massive army, and Winston was worried about the threat that Hitler could become to Britain and the rest of the world.

# The Nazi Threat

**47.** Following the end of World War One, the victorious nations - Britain, France, Russia, and the United States - had punished Germany heavily by making her pay a huge fine and forbidding her to rebuild her Army and Navy.

**48.** Germany was humiliated, and the economy was in ruins with millions of people having no job or money, but a former soldier called Adolf Hitler offered them a solution to their problems.

*Adolf Hitler*

**49.** Hitler was the leader of a political party called the National Socialists - or "Nazis" - and he promised to make Germany great again if the people voted for him.

**50.** Hitler came to power in 1933 and set about rebuilding the Army to go to war again. He planned to build a German empire - the "Third Reich" - which he said would last for 1,000 years.

**51.** Winston was convinced that Hitler would start another war, and he wrote newspaper articles warning of the danger that Germany posed. Most people ignored Winston - one million British soldiers had died in World War One, and nobody wanted another war.

**52.** In March 1938, Hitler began his empire-building by sending his Army over the German border to take over Austria, after which he planned to invade neighboring Czechoslovakia.

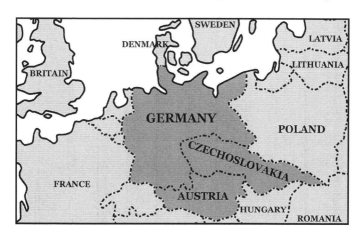

**53.**   When the British Prime Minister, Neville Chamberlain, heard of Hitler's plans for the invasion of Czechoslovakia he flew to Germany to try to talk Hitler out of it. He returned to Britain believing he had succeeded after Hitler promised that Germany would invade no more countries.

**54.**   Winston didn't believe Hitler would keep his word, and he was to be proved right when on September 1, 1939, Germany invaded Poland. Hitler had gone too far this time and two days later Britain declared war on Germany. World War Two had begun.

**55.**   The whole country now realized that Winston had been right about the threat of Germany, and there were calls for him to return to government. Reluctantly, Prime Minister Chamberlain invited Winston to take up his old job as First Lord of the Admiralty. After he had accepted, a message was sent to every ship in the Navy which simply said, "WINSTON IS BACK!"

# The Battle of Britain

**56.** In April 1940, Hitler's Army marched north into Denmark and within hours the country was under German control. Next on Hitler's list was Norway.

**57.**   The British government sent the Navy to help Norway, but the mission was a complete failure. By the middle of June the Germans had seized control of the country.

**58.**   The failure of the British naval campaign to prevent the invasion of Norway brought about the resignation of Neville Chamberlain. He had been an ineffective wartime leader, and the country now needed a strong, energetic Prime Minister to stop Hitler taking over the whole of Europe. That man would be Winston Churchill.

**59.**   Winston became Prime Minister on May 10, 1940, at the age of sixty-five. He felt that his whole life had been leading up to this moment and that it was his destiny to lead his country.

**60.**   During his first month as Prime Minister, Winston saw Hitler invade Holland, Luxembourg, and Belgium before setting his sights on France. On June 14, the German Army entered the French capital, Paris, and a week later France surrendered. Hitler was now planning the invasion of Britain, the country who was standing alone against the might of the German Army and Air Force.

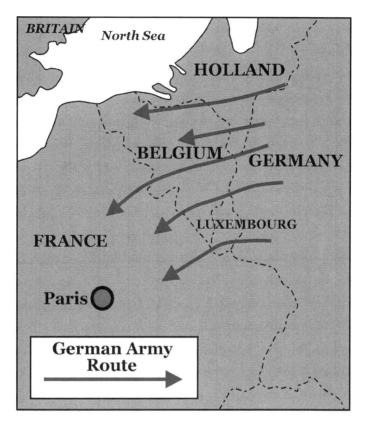

**BRITAIN** North Sea

HOLLAND

BELGIUM

GERMANY

LUXEMBOURG

FRANCE

Paris

German Army Route

---

**61.** Many people in the government thought that Britain should surrender to Hitler while they had the chance, but Winston wouldn't entertain such a thought. He knew that they should stand up to the evil of the Nazis and fight until the bitter end.

**62.** Winston used radio broadcasts to keep the morale of the British people high. His words gave people courage and determination, and the belief that they could defeat Hitler and the Nazis.

*Winston about to broadcast to the nation*

**63.**   In order to invade Britain, Hitler had to send his Army across the English Channel, which separates Britain from France. The ships carrying his soldiers would be easy targets for British fighter aircraft, so Hitler decided that the British Royal Air Force (the RAF) had to be destroyed.

**64.**   During the summer of 1940, the German Air Force - the "Luftwaffe" - and the RAF fought fierce air battles in the skies above southern England. But the Germans failed to destroy the RAF, and decided instead to drop bombs on the cities of Britain.

**65.**   For fifty-seven days and nights, the Luftwaffe dropped bombs on London and other

British cities during what became known as the "Blitz," which is the German word for "lightning." The RAF fought courageously against the Luftwaffe, before the Germans admitted defeat and forced Hitler to abandon his plans to invade Britain.

***Firefighters after a German bombing***

**66.** The RAF lost 400 pilots during the "Battle of Britain," but the country was saved from being taken over by Germany. Winston made a speech in Parliament saluting the pilots of the RAF with the famous words, "Never in the field of human conflict was so much owed by so many to so few."

# The USA Enters the War

**67.** Winston knew that it would be difficult for Britain to defeat Hitler without help. He was desperate for the powerful United States of America to enter the war and fight on Britain's side.

**68.** The United States president, Franklin D. Roosevelt, was a friend of Winston and helped by supplying Britain with weapons and other military equipment. But he refused to commit America to war so soon after the horrors of World War One. Events of December 1941 would change his mind.

*Franklin D. Roosevelt*

**69.** On December 7, 1941, Japan - who was fighting on the same side as Germany - launched a devastating air attack on Pearl Harbor, an American naval base on one of the Hawaiian Islands. Eighteen American warships and nearly 200 aircraft were destroyed, along with the loss of 2,400 lives and 1,000 wounded.

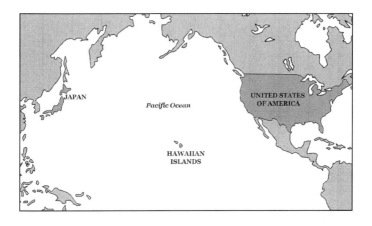

**70.** America was outraged at the attack on Pearl Harbor and declared war on Japan the very next day. Three days later Germany declared war on America. Winston would have preferred the circumstances to have been less tragic, but his wish for America to enter the war had been granted.

**71.** Around the same time as the Pearl Harbor attack, Hitler invaded Russia, bringing another powerful nation into the war against Germany. Britain, the United States, and Russia - known as the "Allies" - along with other countries who had entered the war, were now fighting together and

Winston was convinced that Hitler could now be defeated.

# D-Day & Victory

**72.** With Britain and her allies all fighting together, the tide began to turn against Germany. The Allies began to plan an invasion of Europe so that they could defeat the German Army and march to the German capital, Berlin, where Hitler could be captured.

**73.** The invasion of Europe began on June 6, 1944, when 150,000 British, American, and Canadian soldiers crossed the English Channel to land on the beaches of Normandy in northern France. Even at the age of sixty-six, Winston wanted to be there when the invasion took place, but he was persuaded not to go by King George VI!

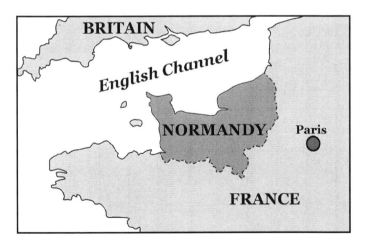

**74.** By the end of June, 850,000 allied soldiers had landed in France to begin the long march to Berlin, fighting the German Army on the way. On the other side of Europe the Russians battled their way to Germany from the east, getting ever closer to Berlin.

**75.** The Russians reached Berlin on April 16, 1945, but were unable to capture Hitler - he had committed suicide before he could be found. Hitler was dead, the German Army was defeated, and the war was nearly over.

**76.** Even though Germany was defeated, Japan kept on fighting. To force them to surrender the Americans dropped an atom bomb on the city of Hiroshima. The bomb was so powerful that 80,000 people were killed instantly and the city was flattened.

*The atom bomb explodes over Hiroshima*

**77.** Three days after Hiroshima the Japanese still hadn't surrendered and a second bomb was dropped, this time on the city of Nagasaki. Five days later, on August 15, 1945, the Japanese finally agreed to surrender. World War Two was over at last.

# After the War

**78.** A general election was held in July 1945, to decide who would lead the country now that the war was over. Winston was confident that the British people would want to keep him as Prime Minister after leading them to victory in World War Two.

**79.** The result of the election came as a real blow to Winston. The Labour Party seemed to have a much better idea of how to rebuild Britain after the war than the Conservatives, and the British people chose Labour to be the new government.

**80.** Winston was now seventy years of age, and Clementine thought that it would be a good time for him to retire. But Winston hated the idea of retirement - he still had plenty of work to do.

**81.** Although not in government, Winston was still an MP and leader of the Conservative Party. The war had made him famous throughout the world and he continued to have an influence on international affairs. In 1946, he traveled to America where he gave a speech warning of the danger coming from Russia.

**82.** Russia was a communist country where the government controls everything and takes freedom away from its people. Following the war, Russia had taken over many countries of

Eastern Europe and forced communism on them.

***Europe after World War Two***

**83.** Winston was afraid that Russia was planning to force communism on the whole of Europe, and eventually even America itself. He warned that there was the danger of yet another world war.

**84.** Many people dismissed Winston's concerns, but he was proved to be right in many ways. From 1945 until 1991, the world would be in the grip of the "Cold War," a war of secrecy, suspicion, and mistrust; when the whole world seemed to be close to destroying itself with weapons of unimaginable power.

**85.**  The general election of 1951 saw a narrow victory for the Conservative Party. Winston was Prime Minister again at the age of seventy-six, and even though he was slowing down he was still devoted to serving his country.

**86.**  Winston suffered a stroke in June 1953, and his health began to decline. He finally decided to resign as Prime Minister in 1955 at the age of seventy-nine.

**87.**  Winston's retirement was spent writing, painting, and traveling; and it lasted for ten years until, on January 15, 1965, he suffered another stroke. He died nine days later on the morning of Sunday, January 24.

**88.**  Winston's funeral was a grand affair, attended by statesmen from all over the world. 350 million people from across the world, including twenty-five million in Britain, watched the funeral on television. He was buried in a churchyard close to Blenheim Palace, where he had been born ninety years earlier.

*Winston Churchill's grave*

# Assorted Winston Churchill Facts

**89.**   Winston first traveled to America in 1895, when he visited New York City. He fell in love with the country and would visit many times during his life, coming to think of it as a second home. In 1963, he was made an honorary citizen of the United States.

**90.**   Winston did a lot to help ordinary people when he was in politics. He made sure that unemployed and sick people got financial help, and that coal miners did not have to work more than eight hours a day. He also saw that prisoners released from prison were given help to improve their lives.

**91.**   Winston and Clementine's beloved Chartwell is now a historic property. It has been restored to look like it would have in the 1920s, and contains the original furniture and books, as well as many of the honors and medals that Churchill received. Thousands of tourists visit Chartwell every year to see how Winston and Clementine would have lived.

**92.**   Winston loved to paint and was especially good at landscape painting. His first painting was "The Garden at Hoe Farm," which was completed in 1915. During his lifetime he painted more than 500 paintings.

**93.**   On one visit to America in 1931, he was hit by a car in New York City. He was in hospital for a long time, but when he recovered he wrote an article for the *Daily Mail* newspaper about his accident. He was paid £600 ($790) and the article was read all over the world.

**94.** On a visit to Cuba in 1895, Winston discovered cigars. They were to become a lifelong love and became part of his image - he was rarely seen without a cigar clenched between his teeth. He even had a special storage room built at Chartwell which held up to 4,000 cigars, all carefully organized and labeled!

# Illustration Attributions

**Title page**
William Timym [Public domain]

**Blenheim Palace**
DeFacto [CC BY-SA 4.0
(https://creativecommons.org/licenses/by-sa/4.0)]

**The First Duke of Marlborough**
Godfrey Kneller [Public domain]
{{PD-US}}

**Lord Randolph and Lady Churchill**
Georges Penabert (Paris) photographe (Arudy,
Pyrénées-Atlantiques, 1825 - Paris, 1903). [Public
domain]
{{PD-US}}

**Winston aged six**
British Government [Public domain]

**Harrow School**
Bernard Burns [CC BY-SA 3.0
(https://creativecommons.org/licenses/by-sa/3.0)]

**Winston in the uniform of the 4th Hussars**
Author unknown [Public domain]

**Winston around the time of his election to
Parliament**
Author unknown [Public domain]

**Clementine Hozier**
Unattributed [Public domain]
{{PD-US}}

**Chartwell**
Gaius Cornelius [CC BY-SA 3.0
(https://creativecommons.org/licenses/by-sa/3.0)]

**Downing Street**
robertsharp [CC BY 2.0
(https://creativecommons.org/licenses/by/2.0)]

**Adolf Hitler**
Bundesarchiv, Bild 183-S33882 / CC BY-SA 3.0 DE
[CC BY-SA 3.0 de
(https://creativecommons.org/licenses/by-
sa/3.0/de/deed.en)]

**Winston about to broadcast to the nation**
War Office official photographer, Egalton (Mr),
Horton (Major) [Public domain]

**Firefighters after a German bombing**
New York Times Paris Bureau Collection [Public
domain]

**Franklin D. Roosevelt**
Author unknown [Public domain]

**The atom bomb explodes over Hiroshima**
509th Operations Group [Public domain]

**Winston Churchill's grave**
Dennis Lloyd [CC BY-SA 3.0
(https://creativecommons.org/licenses/by-sa/3.0)]

**Winston with cigar (Fact 94)**
https://creativecommons.org/publicdomain/mark/
1.0/

Printed in Great Britain
by Amazon

17310536R00027